MEGALOPOLIS

The way people move has changed a lot over the past 800 years! Follow Chester and Christie as they race through time and up the East Coast, trying different forms of transportation along the way. Can they be the first in this treasure hunt to find the "**East Coast Megalopolis**?"

(What IS that, anyway -- a bad horror monster?!!!)

HOW DID PEOPLE LIVE 800 YEARS AGO?

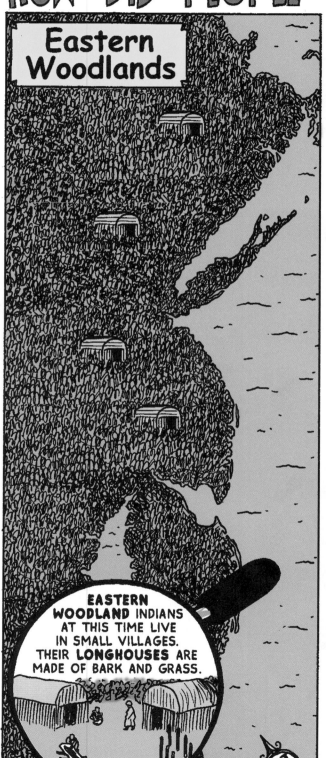

Eastern Woodlands

EASTERN WOODLAND INDIANS AT THIS TIME LIVE IN SMALL VILLAGES. THEIR **LONGHOUSES** ARE MADE OF BARK AND GRASS.

AROUND the COAST in 800 YEARS
CHESUPIOC BAY SHORE

CHESTER, WHAT KIND OF RACE TAKES **800 YEARS**?!!

ONE SET UP TO SHOW YOU HOW LIFE CHANGES. WE WILL RACE ACROSS LAND **AND** TIME!!

BROYD '00

GLAD I'M WEARING MY NEW SNEAKS!

HEY! WHAT KIND OF MOCCASINS ARE THOSE?

NO FAIR! NO FAIR!

YOU WILL **NEED** TO BE FAST TO KEEP UP WITH THESE NATIVE AMERICANS. IN **1200**AD THESE GUYS RUN, WALK, OR PADDLE CANOES WHEREVER THEY NEED TO GO.

THE **GOOD** NEWS, CHRISTIE, IS THAT WE WILL GET TO USE NEW TECHNOLOGY AS WE RACE.

AND WHEN DOES THE MINIVAN GET INVENTED?

NOT UNTIL A LOOOONG TIME FROM NOW.

GO!

RUN, CHESTER! RUN!

RUN, FOREST, RUN!

next: HORSES

HOW FAST WAS MAIL 225 YEARS AGO?

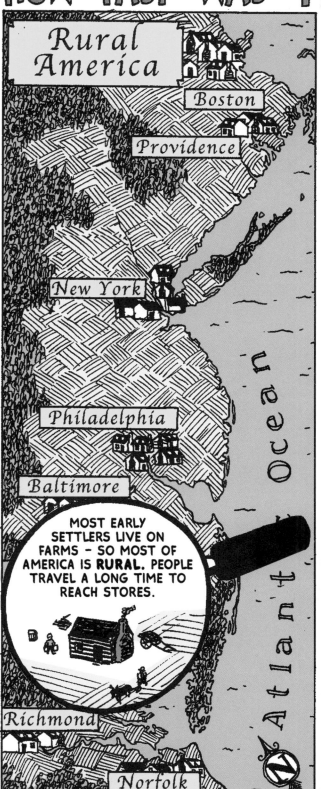

Rural America

Boston

Providence

New York

Philadelphia

Baltimore

Richmond

Norfolk

Atlantic Ocean

MOST EARLY SETTLERS LIVE ON FARMS — SO MOST OF AMERICA IS **RURAL**. PEOPLE TRAVEL A LONG TIME TO REACH STORES.

AROUND the COAST In 800 YEARS

Marathon Station 1 — Alexandria, Va.

HUFF! PUFF!.. HORSES!.. LET'S GET A HORSE!

NOW WE CAN. EUROPEANS BRING HORSES TO THIS PART OF NORTH AMERICA IN THE **1600s**.

WH--? **GEORGE WASHINGTON?!**

YOU MAY USE MY HORSE IF YOU CARRY THIS LETTER TO BOSTON — I MISSED GIVING IT TO THE **BOAT** THAT SAILED BY MY PLANTATION LAST WEEK.

IN THIS ERA, IT TAKES FOUR WEEKS TO GET A LETTER FROM VIRGINIA TO BOSTON. HORSEPATHS GET SO MUDDY IN RAIN THAT THEY BECOME UNUSABLE.

SO LET'S JUST WAIT FOR THE NEXT BOAT.

DEPENDING ON THE WINDS, ANOTHER MAY NOT COME HERE FOR TWO WEEKS.

LET'S KEEP GOING! HEEE**YAAH**

pinch

next: **STEAMBOATS**

HOW DID BOATS GET BETTER IN 1807?

Growth of Port Towns

Boston

Providence

New York

Philadelphia

Richmond

Norfolk

Atlant Ocean

TOWNS GROW ALONG RIVERS. SHIPS ARE THE FASTEST AND EASIEST WAY TO MOVE THINGS IN THIS TIME.

AROUND the COAST In 800 YEARS
MARATHON STATION No 2 ~ BALTIMORE, MD.

WHOOAH! THAT WAS A **LOT** FASTER THAN WALKING!!

BUT NOW OUR HORSE IS TIRED. ALL HUMAN AND ANIMAL RESOURCES GET TIRED FROM WORK.

WHAT WE NEED IS AN **ENGINE** THAT NEVER STOPS.

HERE COMES ONE NOW! **ROBERT FULTON** JUST PUT A STEAM ENGINE ON THAT BOAT. NOW IT CAN **TRAVEL ANYTIME**, INSTEAD OF DEPENDING ON WIND LIKE SAILING SHIPS.

SOUTHERN FARMERS USE STEAMBOATS TO SHIP COTTON TO NORTHERN FACTORIES.

ALL I CARE ABOUT IS WINNING THIS RACE!! LET'S GET TO PHIL-A-DELPHIA

next: **TRAINS**

4

HOW DID WE GET INTO THIS JAM?

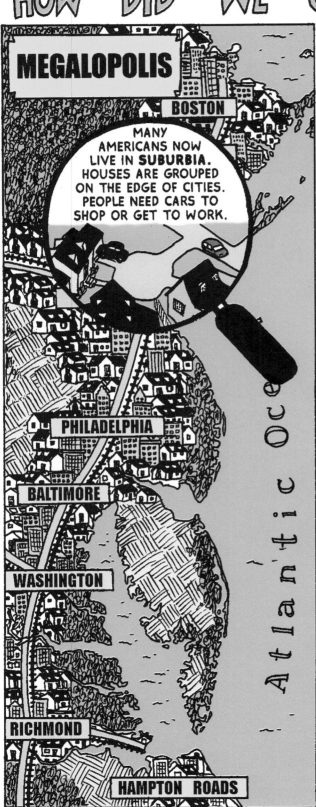

MEGALOPOLIS

BOSTON

MANY AMERICANS NOW LIVE IN **SUBURBIA**. HOUSES ARE GROUPED ON THE EDGE OF CITIES. PEOPLE NEED CARS TO SHOP OR GET TO WORK.

PHILADELPHIA

BALTIMORE

WASHINGTON

RICHMOND

HAMPTON ROADS

Atlantic Ocean

AROUND the COAST In 800 YEARS

MARATHON STATION 4: NEW YORK

ALMOST TO THE BOSTON FINISH! **WHERE IS OUR MINIVAN?!**

HERE! AND, JUST AS IMPORTANT, THERE IS THE **INTERSTATE HIGHWAY RAMP!**

INTERSTATE ROADS ARE BUILT IN THE **1960s**. THEY REPLACE RAILROADS AS THE MAIN LINK BETWEEN CITIES. FOUR-LANE ROADS AND FAMILY CARS GIVE PEOPLE MORE **SPEED** AND **CONVENIENCE.**

BOYD '08

CITIES SPREAD OUT EVEN MORE, ALONG THE INTERSTATE'S PATH.

MORE CARS, MORE CITIES — HEY, HAVE WE LEFT NEW YORK CITY YET?

IT IS HARD TO TELL! THE INTERSTATE TIES TOGETHER A STRING OF CITIES ALONG THE ATLANTIC COAST. THE ONES WE PASSED THROUGH ON THIS RACE ARE NOW PART OF **"THE NORTHEAST MEGALOPOLIS"**!!

IT JUST LOOKS LIKE ONE BIG TRAFFIC JAM! LET'S GET AN **AIRPLANE!** LET'S GO TO THE AIRPORT!

THIS **IS** THE ROAD TO THE AIRPORT!

Hmmm, MAYBE WE SHOULD GET OUT AND WALK... END

MOVING IN 1902

Let's take a look at the different forms of transportation people had in one year of history. Watch how fast and how far Chester can move using horses, boats, trains, and something NEW in 1902 . . .

HOW FAR CAN A PERSON WALK IN A DAY?

HI, TAMARA!

HI, CHESTER.

WHERE ARE YOU GOING?

NOT VERY FAR OR FAST ON **THESE** LITTLE LEGS!

CAN I GIVE YOU A RIDE?

THANKS! NOW I'LL GET THIS LETTER DELIVERED MUCH FASTER.

HOW FAR ARE WE TAKING IT?

OH, A HUMAN CAN WALK ABOUT 20 MILES IN A DAY.

20 MILES?

BOYD '02

THAT'S WHAT WE'RE LIMITED TO — UNLESS YOU HAVE A CAR, BOAT, HORSE, OR AIRCRAFT.

I DON'T HAVE ANY OF THOSE!

THAT MAKES YOU LIKE MOST AMERICANS IN THE EARLY 1900s. ALL THOSE VEHICLES ARE EXPENSIVE OR RARE. WALKING IS THE MAIN TRANSPORTATION.

"TRANSPORTERS"?

NONONO — **TRANSPORTATION!** WAYS WE GET AROUND! WAYS TO MOVE GOODS AND SERVICES! PLANES, TRAINS, AND AUTOMOBILES!!

CHESTER AND TAMARA ARRIVE IN RICHMOND.

HERE IS YOUR LETTER, MR. MARTIN.

WH— I DON'T BELIEVE IT!

next: a Horse of Course

HOW FAR CAN HORSES TRAVEL IN A DAY?

CHESTER AND THIRD-GRADER TAMARA JUST WALKED A LETTER TO RICHMOND IN 1902...

JUMPIN' JEHOSAPHAT!

THIS LETTER SAYS I MUST GET THREE BARRELS OF TOBACCO TO BALTIMORE IN **THREE** DAYS!

CAN YOU TWO GET IT THERE FOR ME?

DEPENDS. WHAT KIND OF TRANSPORTATION DO YOU HAVE IN MIND?

I AM **NOT** WALKING AGAIN!

GET MY BEST HORSE AND A WAGON!

YEEEHA!

CHESTER AND TAMARA AND THE HORSE COVER ABOUT 50 MILES IN ONE DAY!

OOP! AH! OW

THESE DIRT ROADS ARE A BIT ROUGH..

HORSES ALSO GET **TIRED**. ANIMAL MUSCLES NEED TO REST SOONER OR LATER. *PHEW!!*

HEY, YOU GOT US TO THE BOAT LANDING! WE CAN SWITCH TO A STEADY MACHINE OF STEAM!

NEXT: **STEAMBOAT WILLY**

CHESTER THE CRAB
WHAT DID THE BALTIMORE BOATS CARRY?

CHESTER AND THIRD-GRADER TAMARA ARE SHIPPING THREE BARRELS IN 1902...

AH... I'M GLAD ... WE'RE OFF THE WAGON. ⸨HUFF!⸩ THOSE COUNTRY ROADS WERE A MUDDY MESS!

FOR VIRGINIA TOWNS NEAR THE CHESAPEAKE BAY, IT IS EASIER IN THESE DAYS TO GET SUPPLIES BY BOAT THAN BY WAGON. THERE ARE MORE THAN 200 BOAT LANDINGS ALONG THE BAY.

CHECKING THREE BARRELS OF TOBACCO UP TO BALTIMORE?

YES.

AND ONE CRAB.

HEY!

CRABS

I THOUGHT OUR TICKETS WERE FOR FIRST CLASS ...

CRABS

BOYD '02

STEAMBOATS HAVE BEEN ON THE BAY SINCE THE WEEMS BROTHERS FIRST RAN ONE FROM BALTIMORE TO THE PATUXENT RIVER IN MARYLAND IN 1817. BY 1902, STEAMBOATS CARRY PEOPLE, SEAFOOD, FURNITURE, TOOLS, STOVES, AND CLOTHES ALL OVER THE BAY.

Mitchell & Sons
BALTIMORE

THAT WAS FUN!

THESE BOATS TRANSPORT (CARRY) A LOT, QUICKLY. THAT COW FROM VIRGINIA WILL BE PROCESSED HERE AND SHIPPED BACK TO BE SOLD IN VIRGINIA STORES IN A FEW DAYS.

next: HONEST ENGINE

CHESTER THE CRAB
HOW FAST WERE TRAINS IN 1902?

CHESTER AND TAMARA ARE IN BALTIMORE IN **1902**.

GOOD JOB GETTING THE TOBACCO HERE BY THE DEADLINE. HERE IS MR. MARTIN'S PAYMENT.

IT NEEDS TO BE IN HIS BANK ACCOUNT IN NEW YORK CITY **TOMORROW**.

JUST SEND IT YOURSELF! WIRE IT IN A TELEGRAM!!

THE TELEGRAPH **IS** A FAST WAY TO COMMUNICATE. BUT THIS CHECK IS IMPORTANT ENOUGH THAT IT SHOULD BE HAND-DELIVERED.

OR EVEN **CLAW-**DELIVERED.

CHESTER AND TAMARA BOARD A RAILROAD TRAIN.

AT LEAST WE GET TO TAKE A FAST TRAIN.

TRAINS ARE FASTER THAN WALKING, RIDING HORSES, OR TAKING A SHIP. PLUS, THEY CARRY MORE STUFF THAN A HORSE.

THE DRAWBACK IS THAT I GO ONLY CERTAIN PLACES. I CAN'T GET OFF MY RAILS. **BOTHER THAT!**

A LOT OF TRACK HAS BEEN BUILT SINCE THE FIRST STEAM ENGINE IN AMERICA ROLLED IN PENNSYLVANIA IN 1829. BY 1902 THERE ARE ABOUT 193,000 MILES OF TRACK ACROSS THE NATION. TRAINS CAN CARRY PEOPLE, PIGS, POTTERY, PILLOWS . . .

ALL AT 60 MILES PER HOUR!

next: **READY TEDDY**

BOYD '02

11

WHO WAS THE 1ST PRESIDENT IN A CAR?

CHESTER AND TAMARA HAVE TAKEN A TRAIN TO NEW YORK CITY IN 1902.

HERE IS THE CHECK FOR MR. MARTIN'S BANK ACCOUNT.

THANK YOU, YOUNG LADY.

THAT FINISHES MY BUSINESS FOR TODAY. NOW I CAN DRIVE MY NEW HORSELESS CARRIAGE TO SEE THE PRESIDENT. WOULD YOU LIKE TO COME?

SO THIS TIME OUR TRANSPORTATION WILL CARRY...

US!

CLOSED

THIS IS A ...CAR??!

WHERE IS THE MP3 PLAYER?

THIS IS AN OLDSMOBILE. RANSOM OLDS HAS BEEN MAKING THEM SINCE 1897. IT CARRIES FIVE GALLONS OF GASOLINE AND COST ME $650.

THE TRAIN WAS FASTER.

CARS CAN GO PLACES TRAINS CANNOT. EACH FORM OF TRANSPORTATION FITS DIFFERENT NEEDS.

DESPITE BUMPY ROADS, THE OLDSMOBILE TRIO REACHES HARTFORD, CONNECTICUT, IN TIME TO SEE:

TEDDY ROOSEVELT!!

ON AUG. 22, 1902, ROOSEVELT BECOMES THE FIRST UNITED STATES PRESIDENT TO RIDE IN AN AUTOMOBILE.

THIS IS A GREAT WAY OF TRANSPORTATION! NOW I CAN SHAKE HANDS EVEN FASTER!!

(SAYS THE GUY WHO ONCE RODE A MOOSE IN A LAKE!)

WHO TOLD YOU ABOUT THE MOOSE??!

BOYD '02

END

CHAPTER 3

WRIGHT FLIGHT

Two brothers from Ohio are late in joining the Turn-of-the-Century craze to put man in the air. But moving carefully and logically the Wright Brothers begin to solve some of the basic problems to powered flight . . .

CHESTER THE CRAB

1879
EDISON'S LIGHT

1896

1914
WORLD WAR I

HOW CAN WINGS LIFT THINGS?

DOZENS OF INVENTORS ARE TRYING TO BUILD THE **FIRST AIRPLANE** IN THE LATE 1800s. A GERMAN NAMED OTTO LILIENTHAL FLIES A GLIDER ALMOST 2,000 TIMES TO TEST HIS IDEAS, UNTIL...

I-I CAN'T CONTROL IT! AAAAAAAAAAAAA

NEWS OF LILIENTHAL'S DEATH REACHES **ORVILLE AND WILBUR WRIGHT** IN DAYTON, OHIO, IN **1896**.

Dayton News
LILIENTHAL DIES
WILL MAN EVER FLY??

ORVILLE, WE CAN DO BETTER!

THEY KNOW WHERE TO BEGIN THIS PROJECT...

THE LIBRARY!!

Stringfellow

Sir George Cayley

Chitty Chitty Bang Bang

Peter Pan

Da Vinci

THE BOOKS POINT TO SOMETHING CALLED "**LIFT**." LILIENTHAL SHAPED HIS GLIDER WINGS LIKE A BIRD'S WING TO GET LIFT.

A WING DIVIDES THE AIR. A CHANGE IN THE DIRECTION OR SPEED OF THE AIR FLOW MEANS THERE IS **ACCELERATION**. THAT ACCELERATION CAUSES A CHANGE IN PRESSURE BETWEEN THE TOP AND BOTTOM OF THE WING. (THIS CAN ALSO WORK ON A FLAT WING IF IT DIVIDES THE AIR AT AN ANGLE.)

LIFT LIFT LIFT

THE STRONGER AIR PRESSURE **UNDER** THE WING PUSHES THE WING UP. THIS CREATES LIFT!

WOULD THIS WORK ON A CLAW??

BIRDS HAVE SOMETHING LILIENTHAL DID NOT: **CONTROL**. FLYING WITHOUT CONTROL IS CRAZY! HOW CAN **WE** GET CONTROL??

next:
SWITCHING TO GLIDE

HOW DID THE WRIGHTS CONTROL FLIGHT?

HOW LONG WAS THE 1ST WRIGHT FLIGHT?

Wilbur and Orville Wright return to Kill Devil Hills, North Carolina, in **1903**. They have a glider with a motor they built themselves in their bicycle shop in Dayton, Ohio.

HAVE YOU HEARD? SAMUEL PIERPONT LANGLEY'S AERODROME JUST **CRASHED** INTO THE POTOMAC RIVER. HE FAILED TO FLY!

OUCH! THAT CRAFT COST $73,000.

WE'VE SPENT ONLY $1,000 ON OURS! LET'S GET GOING BEFORE WINTER HITS.

ON DEC. 17, PUDDLES AROUND THEIR CAMP ARE FROZEN. WINDS ARE HIGH.

LET'S DO IT.

ORVILLE CLIMBS ABOARD. THE "WRIGHT FLYER" CLATTERS DOWN A 60-FOOT RAIL.

KLAKLIKLAKLACKLIKLAKLAKLAKKKKLAK

BBOYD '02

HE FLIES!

HE GOES 120 FEET IN 12 SECONDS — ABOUT THE TIME IT TAKES TO SAY:

THIS IS THE FIRST FLIGHT BY A HEAVIER-THAN-AIR MACHINE CARRYING A PERSON THAT

- RAISES ITSELF BY ITS OWN POWER
- SAILS FORWARD WITHOUT SLOWING
- LANDS AT A POINT AS HIGH AS IT STARTED!

THIS FIRST FLIGHT ISN'T FAR, BUT IT POINTS THE WAY TO SPACE SHUTTLES!

END

CHAPTER 4

INTERSTATE HIGHWAYS

There wasn't always a Burger King off every exit of I-70. The roadways for cars grew slowly as people and politicians figured out how important the car would be in America's culture and economy. After decades of muddy rural roads and narrow paved state routes, a president pushes for the breakthrough in wheeled transportation . . .

WHAT WERE ROADS LIKE IN 1903?

GOOD MORNING, DARYLLE! ARE YOU READY TO DO YOUR SCHOOL PROJECT ON ROADS?

Hmm? Oh, ROADS. Yeah. uh-huh

Krunk Krunk Krunk

:SNAP:

CRACKLE

POP

HEY, WHAT HAPPENED TO MY CHOCO-FROSTED SUGAR SMAKDOWNS!? AND MY ORANGE JUICE!!?

YOUR ORANGE IS STILL ON A TREE IN FLORIDA. **THIS** IS WHAT YOUR LIFE WOULD BE LIKE 100 YEARS AGO.

DARYLLE! TIME TO GO TO SCHOOL!

BOYD '03

IN **1903**, THERE IS NO SCHOOL BUS FOR YOUR NEIGHBORHOOD, EITHER.

HUH. I CAN STILL RIDE MY BIKE THOUGH, RIGHT?

YOU CAN **TRY!**

GRUNT ARRRG!!

MY WHEELS WON'T TURN IN THIS **MUD!** THIS ROAD IS A **MESS** WHEN IT RAINS!

IN 1903 THERE ARE ABOUT 2.4 MILLION MILES OF ROADS IN THE UNITED STATES. ONLY 9 PERCENT OF THEM HAVE A HARD SURFACE.

THIS IS THE STREET?!

YES, LOCAL GOVERNMENT IS IN CHARGE OF THIS ROAD BUT SPENDS LITTLE MONEY TO FIX IT. BICYCLISTS ARE STARTING A "GOOD ROADS MOVEMENT" TO CHANGE THAT!

NEXT: DRIVE THE USA

WHO IS FIRST TO DRIVE ACROSS AMERICA?

WHAT ROAD WENT COAST-TO-COAST 1ST?

CHESTER AND FIRST-GRADER DARYLLE HAVE MET A FARMER IN **1903**...

THE RAILROAD IS TOO EXPENSIVE. I CAN'T GET MY CROPS TO MARKET THAT WAY.

WHAT DO YOU GROW?

CORN AND APPLES, MOSTLY.

YUM! I'M HUNGRY FROM WALKING. MAY I HAVE AN APPLE, PLEASE?

I WON'T HAVE APPLES UNTIL THEY RIPEN IN THE FALL.

BUT — BUT I HAVE AN APPLE FOR SNACK EVERY DAY.

DARYLLE, THE REASON **YOU** GET APPLES YEAR-ROUND IS THAT THEY GET FLOWN, SHIPPED, AND DRIVEN ALL OVER THE WORLD. IF APPLES ARE RIPE IN AUSTRALIA IN MAY, THEY GET TRANSPORTED TO YOUR STORE IN MAY!

IN **1903**, MOST OF WHAT YOU EAT IS WHAT YOU CAN FIND LOCALLY. HAVE A ROADSIDE RASPBERRY.

IN **1908**, **HENRY FORD** BEGINS MAKING A CHEAP, STURDY CAR — THE MODEL T. MANY PEOPLE BUY THEM. IN 1910 THERE ARE 470,000 CARS IN AMERICA; BY 1920 THERE ARE NINE MILLION!

HANK

BBOYD '03

YOU CAN HAVE THEM IN ANY COLOR YOU WANT, AS LONG AS IT IS BLACK.

THE MILLIONS OF NEW DRIVERS PRESSURE POLITICIANS TO PAY FOR BETTER ROADS. IN **1916** THE UNITED STATES CONGRESS SETS UP A SYSTEM TO DO THAT. THE FEDERAL GOVERNMENT WILL MATCH MONEY THAT STATES SPEND ON ROADS.

AMERICA'S **FIRST** COAST-TO-COAST ROAD IS THE **LINCOLN HIGHWAY**. ITS 3,384 MILES FROM NEW YORK TO SAN FRANCISCO ARE PAVED DURING THE 1910s AND 1920s.

2-391

next: DRIVE THRU

WHEN DID INTERSTATES CONNECT STATES?

PEOPLE WANT TO SPEED UP AND SMOOTH OUT AMERICA'S CAR TRAFFIC. THEIR ANSWER IS TO BUILD WIDER ROADS, DIVIDED BY A GRASS STRIP, WITH NO STOPLIGHTS AND ONLY A FEW RAMPS TO GET ON AND OFF.

CONNECTICUT BUILDS THE MERRITT PARKWAY, FINISHING IN 1940.

WOW, FOUR LANES FROM NEW YORK TO NEW HAVEN!!

CHICAGO TURNS LAKE SHORE DRIVE FROM A PARK PATH INTO AN EXPRESSWAY.

WOW! EIGHT LANES!

THE PENNSYLVANIA TURNPIKE STRETCHES THIS IDEA 360 MILES ACROSS THE WHOLE STATE. ITS FIRST MODERN SECTION OPENS IN 1940.

PENNA TURNPIKE

I CAN GO 90 MPH!!

UNITED STATES PRESIDENT AND FORMER GENERAL **DWIGHT D. EISENHOWER** USES FEDERAL MONEY TO TIE THESE ROADS TOGETHER INTO ONE BIG **INTERSTATE HIGHWAY** SYSTEM. ("INTERSTATE" MEANS BETWEEN STATES.)

WE'LL GET 42,000 MILES OF ROADS THAT ARE WIDE ENOUGH TO CARRY TANKS, MISSILES—AND STATION WAGONS, OF COURSE.

DOES ANYONE KNOW WHICH LOOP WE'RE ON?!

Wheeee!

IN **1956**, CONGRESS BUDGETS $32 BILLION FOR THIS—THE LARGEST GOVERNMENT BUILDING PROJECT UP TO THAT TIME.

THE FIRST NEWLY-CONSTRUCTED SECTION OF IKE'S INTERSTATE IS FINISHED IN 1964. IT IS I-495, THE BELTWAY CIRCLING THE NATION'S CAPITAL, **WASHINGTON, D.C.**

YAYY! WE'RE ALMOST TO GRAMMY'S HOUSE! THIS IS THE ROAD WE USUALLY TAKE!

THIS IS THE ROAD WE ARE **ALL** ON NOW. THE 40 YEARS OF IKE'S PLAN HAVE SEEN PEOPLE AND PRODUCTS MOVE FASTER AND FASTER—EXCEPT WHEN THEY HIT TRAFFIC JAMS. WHAT WILL THE NEXT TRANSPORTATION IDEA BE? END